Follow Me Around™
Cuba

By Michael Bell

SCHOLASTIC

Content Consultant:
Lillian Guerra, PhD
Professor of Cuban & Caribbean History
University of Florida
Gainesville, Florida

Library of Congress Cataloging-in-Publication Data
Names: Bell, Michael, 1965- author.
Title: Cuba / by Michael Bell.
Description: New York, NY : Children's Press, an imprint of Scholastic Inc., [2018] |
Series: Follow me around | Includes bibliographical references and index.
Identifiers: LCCN 2017050083 | ISBN 9780531129173 (library binding) | ISBN 9780531138595 (pbk.)
Subjects: LCSH: Cuba—Description and travel—Juvenile literature. | Cuba—Social life and customs—Juvenile literature.
Classification: LCC F1758.5 .B54 2018 | DDC 917.29104—dc23
LC record available at https://lccn.loc.gov/2017050083

Design: Judith Christ Lafond & Anna Tunick Tabachnik
Text: Wiley Blevins
© 2019 Scholastic Inc.

All rights reserved. Published in 2019 by Children's Press, an imprint of Scholastic Inc.
Printed in North Mankato, MN, USA 113
SCHOLASTIC, CHILDREN'S PRESS, and associated logos are trademarks and/or registered trademarks of Scholastic Inc.
Scholastic Inc., 557 Broadway, New York, NY 10012

1 2 3 4 5 6 7 8 9 10 R 28 27 26 25 24 23 22 21 20 19

Photos ©:cover background: Bella Falk/Alamy Images; cover children: PeopleImages/iStockphoto; back cover: PeopleImages/iStockphoto; 1: PeopleImages/iStockphoto; 3: ullstein bild - Wodicka/The Granger Collection; 4 top left background: Alan Copson/Getty Images; 4 children: PeopleImages/iStockphoto; 6 left: J Marshall - Tribaleye Images/Alamy Images; 6 right: Roberto Machado Noa/LightRocket/Getty Images; 7 top: manoa/Getty Images; 7 bottom: possohh/Shutterstock; 8 left: Roberto Machado Noa/LightRocket/Getty Images; 8 right: Russ Schleipman/Getty Images; 9 top left: STR/AFP/Getty Images; 9 top center: bonchan/iStockphoto; 9 top right: apeinado/iStockphoto; 9 center: MychkoAlezander/iStockphoto; 9 bottom: Yukari Kida/EyeEm/Getty Images; 10: YAMIL LAGE/AFP/Getty Images; 12 left: yupiramos/age fotostock; 12 top right roach: ARTYuSTUDIO/Shutterstock; 12 top right clothes: Sundra/Shutterstock; 12 bottom right: CSA-Printstock/Getty Images; 12-13 music notes: Dejan Popovic/Shutterstock; 12-13 background: Vadim Yerofeyev/Dreamstime; 13 left: Tanya Syrytsyna/Shutterstock; 13 right: Art Alex/Shutterstock; 14 top left: Danita Delimont/Getty Images; 14 top right: Jon Arnold/Getty Images; 14 bottom: Kamira/Shutterstock; 15 left: Craig Lovell/Getty Images; 15 right: Ernesto Tereñes/iStockphoto; 16 left: van der Meer Marica/age fotostock; 16 right: Nikada/iStockphoto; 16 bottom: ullstein bild - Wodicka/The Granger Collection; 17 left: USO/iStockphoto; 17 right: Raul Touzon/Getty Images; 18 left: Everett Historica/Shutterstock; 18 center: Mithra - Index/The Image Works; 18 right: Janusz Pienkowski/Shutterstock; 19 center: ZUMA Press, Inc./Newscom; 19 right: ADALBERTO ROQUE/AFP/Getty Images; 19 left: Nawrocki/ClassicStock/Getty Images; 20 top left: fotoember/iStockphoto; 20 bottom: sunsetman/Shutterstock; 21 bottom left: stockstudioX/iStockphoto; 21 right: Phil Clarke Hill/In Pictures Ltd./Corbis/Getty Images; 21 top left: Bella Falk/Alamy Images; 22 left: Stephen Smith/Alamy Images; 22 right: Glenn Bartley/BIA/Minden Pictures; 23 top: Roberto Machado Noa/LightRocket/Getty Images; 23 center top: Sven Creutzmann/Mambo Photography/Getty Images; 23 center bottom: YAMIL LAGE/AFP/Getty Images; 23 bottom: Ruth Hofshi/Alamy Images; 24 top: Atlantide Phototravel/Getty Images; 24 bottom: Ryan Pierse/Getty Images; 25 right: Roberto Machado Noa/LightRocket/Getty Images; 25 left: Teo Moreno Moreno/Alamy Images; 26 top left: robertharding/Superstock, Inc.; 26 top right: dbimages/Alamy Images; 26 bottom: Mirko Zanni/Getty Images; 27 top left: Harvepino/iStockphoto; 27 center left: Jorge Rey/Newsmakers/Getty Images; 27 bottom left: Cagan H. Sekercioglu/Getty Images; 27 right: Roberto Machado Noa/LightRocket/Getty Images; 28 A.: LatitudeStock/Alamy Images; 28 C.: Everett Collection; 28 D.: venemama/iStockphoto; 28 E.: MindStorm/Shutterstock; 28 F.: Richard Cavalleri/Shutterstock; 28 G.: Roberto Machado Noa/LightRocket/Getty Images; 29: thumb/Getty Images; 30 top right: Kriangx1234/Shutterstock; 30 top left: Leontura/Getty Images; 30 bottom: PeopleImages/iStockphoto.

Maps by Jim McMahon/Mapman ®.

**Front cover:
Paseo Martí
in Havana**

2

Table of Contents

Where in the World Is Cuba?

Hola (OH-lah) from Cuba! That's how we say "hello." I'm Isa, and this is Luis, my best friend. We're your tour guides. Welcome to our island country. Look at a map and you'll see that our country is shaped like a *caimán* (kye-MAHN). That's a small alligator. Its head juts out into the Atlantic Ocean, and its tail points toward Mexico.

Cuba is located in the Caribbean Sea, off the coast of North America. It's the largest island in the Caribbean. There is a lot to show you. *¡Vámonos* (VAH-moh-nohs)*!* Let's go!

Fast Facts:

- Cuba covers 42,804 square miles (110,862 square kilometers).

- The island lies 90 miles (145 km) south of Florida.

- Cuba is part of a chain of islands called the West Indies.

- About 4,000 smaller islands surrounding the island of Cuba are part of the country.

- Cuba has more than 200 rivers, many of which dry up during the dry season.

- Cuba's nearest neighbors are the United States, Mexico, the Bahamas, and the island of Hispaniola. Hispaniola is home to two countries: Haiti and the Dominican Republic.

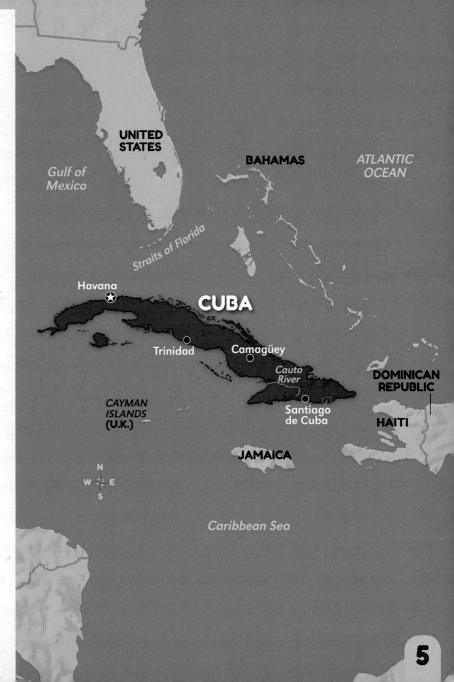

UNITED STATES

Gulf of Mexico

BAHAMAS

ATLANTIC OCEAN

Straits of Florida

Havana

CUBA

Trinidad

Camagüey

Cauto River

DOMINICAN REPUBLIC

CAYMAN ISLANDS (U.K.)

Santiago de Cuba

HAITI

JAMAICA

N W E S

Caribbean Sea

Giant blue barrels hold extra water for the times when the water system shuts down.

Home Sweet Home

Our home is Havana, Cuba. Both of us live in the same apartment building. Luis lives with his parents in one apartment. I live down the hall in an apartment with my mom, grandparents, aunt, and cousins. For a long time, the Cuban government did not allow people to buy or sell homes. So, most Cubans lived with their parents and other family. But the law recently changed. My *madre* (MAH-dray, mom) is saving to buy us our own home!

We spend a lot of time outside riding bikes and playing baseball.

Luis's grandparents live in the country, where they farm. His *abuela* (ah-BWEH-lah, grandmother) is strict about manners. She makes sure we always say "*por favor*" (por fah-VOR, please) and "*gracias*" (GRAH-see-ahs, thank you). She's also a great cook! Luis's *abuelo* (ah-BWEH-loh, grandfather) says she makes the best *empanada* (ehm-pah-NAH-dah) in all of Cuba!

Apartment building in Camagüey

Some Cubans live in small houses. But there are also many apartment buildings. The government built them many years ago. At times, life is challenging in the apartments. Nearly everyone has electricity and running water. Sometimes we lose electricity and our water pumps stop working—maybe for days!—because the government doesn't have enough funds. We plan ahead by filling water tanks and buying candles if we can. But hotels and restaurants for tourists usually have electricity and water all the time.

Getting Creative

Things are often in short supply in Cuba. Certain foods, such as vegetables or beef, are rarely available. When a car or bike breaks down, we don't always have new parts to fix it. So when times get tough, we get creative. For example, people here know how to keep car engines running for decades. My mom still drives my great-grandfather's car! And we never waste anything if we can help it. Every object has another use, from using a food can for storage to turning old toothpaste tubes into a new purse.

Dinner

Plantains

Let's Eat!

In Cuba, we rarely eat in restaurants because we can't afford the prices. Instead, we prefer to gather at someone's home and make a party of it. Most fruits and vegetables are not always available or affordable. But one exception is plantains. These are common and delicious! The plantain looks a lot like a banana. My mom cuts it into thin slices and fries it. Yum! We call this dish *chicharritas* (chee-chah-REE-tahs). Thick slices are called *tostones* (tohs-TOH-nehs). They are a popular snack. In the early summer, we get a particularly tasty treat—mangoes! This is when mangoes are ripe. We look forward to having a sweet, juicy mango at this time all year.

We also eat a lot of corn, black beans, and rice. Beef is very rare and highly prized. But chicken is sometimes eaten, especially in *arroz con pollo* (AH-rohz kohn POH-yoh), rice with chicken.

Cleaning rice

Tostones

Café con leche

Arroz con pollo

Flan

Preparing supper is a family affair. One task we all share is cleaning the rice. Like many supplies and services in Cuba, the government sells us rice at low prices. This is to keep food more easily affordable. In many other countries, the rice is cleaned before being packaged and sold in the store. This can be expensive. To save money, the government buys rice that hasn't been cleaned. So, each evening, we sit together and pick out pebbles and other bits from the rice. Then we rinse and cook it. As we work, we talk, joke, and gossip about our day. In a big family, it can get pretty loud!

Coffee is a major crop here. Adults drink *café con leche* (kah-FEH kohn LEH-cheh)—coffee with warm milk. It's delicious! Speaking of delicious, *flan* (FLAHN) is a favorite dessert. This sweet custard has a glaze of candied sugar.

We always wear uniforms in school.

Off to School

In Cuba, public school is free. University is, too. We must go to school from the ages of 6 to 16. After that, we can choose to continue for three more years. During this time, we study a particular subject or prepare for a job. This might be teacher training, fine arts, **agriculture**, or other topics. Our school year is a little longer than it is in the United States. Ours lasts from September to July.

Luis and I walk to school each day with a group of our *compañeros* (kohm-pahn-YEHR-ohs), or friends. In Cuba, it's important to work together as "comrades." Working together has helped us build a strong nation. In school, we wear the red-and-white uniforms and red scarf of the Pioneers for **Communism**. After sixth grade, our uniform's color changes depending on the grade or school.

One of the things we learn is how to read and write Spanish. Almost everyone can read and write. We also learn English. Some words in these two languages are very similar to each other!

If you're learning Spanish, you might be tripped up by the double r (rr). To speak it, you roll the r. It sounds like a car motor starting up. Rest your tongue behind your front teeth and let it vibrate. Try it!

You probably already know some Spanish words!

English	Spanish
delicious	**delicioso** (deh-lee-see-OH-soh)
correct	**correcto** (kor-REHK-toh)
fantastic	**fantástico** (fahn-TAHS-tee-koh)
rapid	**rápido** (RAH-pee-doh)
important	**importante** (eem-por-TAHN-teh)
difference	**diferencia** (dee-feh-REHN-see-ah)

Knowing how to count to 10 is important when you visit Cuba. Practice and you'll be an expert!

1   uno *(OO-noh)*

2   **dos** *(DOHS)*

3   tres *(TRAYS)*

4   **cuatro** *(KWAH-troh)*

5   **cinco** *(SEEN-koh)*

6   **seis** *(SAYS)*

7   **siete** *(SYEH-teh)*

8   **ocho** *(OH-choh)*

9   nueve *(NWEH-veh)*

10   **diez** *(dee-EHS)*

Cucarachita Martina

In school, we read a lot of traditional tales. One of the most famous is the story of a little cockroach named Martina.

Once upon a time, there lived a sweet cockroach named Cucarachita Martina. One day, she found a gold coin. "This is more money than I have ever seen," she said. "What will I buy? Candy? No. Jewelry? No. Sweet-scented powder? Yes!" And so she did.

That night, Martina powdered herself with her fancy new perfume. She put on her most beautiful dress. Then she sat outside her home feeling rather pretty and sweet-smelling.

Mr. Cat, Señor Gato, slinked by. "Martina, you are so beautiful today. Will you marry me?"

"Let me hear how you sing," said Martina. "Then I will consider it."

"Miau . . . Miau . . . Miauuu," sang Mr. Cat.

"Oh no," said Martina. "That sound frightens me."

Mr. Cat sadly walked away.

A bit later, Mr. Toad, Señor Sapo, hopped by. "Martina, you are so beautiful today. Will you marry me?"

"Let me hear how you sing," she said. "Then I will consider it."

"Crr-oak . . . Crr-oak . . . Crr-oak," sang Mr. Toad.

"Oh no," said Martina. "That sound frightens me." Mr. Toad sadly walked away.

Then a little mouse named Ratoncito Pérez walked by. He was quite shy and polite. He bowed to greet Martina. Then he said in his softest voice, "Martina, you are so beautiful today. Will you marry me?"

"Let me hear how you sing," she said. "Then I will consider it."

"Choo-ee . . . Choo-ee . . . Choo-ee," sang Pérez. Martina loved the sound so much that she married him the next day!

One evening, Martina began cooking her husband's favorite onion soup. "I am going to the store to buy more spices," she said. "Please watch the soup on the stove. But don't eat it yet!"

While she was away, little Pérez grew hungry. He spotted a tasty-looking bit of onion floating in the soup. He reached for it, but leaned over too far and fell in.

SPLASH!

When Martina returned, she found her husband in the pot. "Oh no!" she cried. "Pérez has drowned!" Then she began singing in her saddest voice about her poor Pérez. If only he had waited for the soup to be ready!

Old Havana

Touring Cuba

Havana: Capital City

Welcome to our city, Havana. We Cubans call it, la Habana. It's the capital of Cuba. We have many wonderful sites. If you visit, head to Revolution Square. The National Library and National Theater are both there. You'll also spot the giant statue of José Martí, a hero of our country.

After that, head over to a section of town called Old Havana. There you'll see pastel-painted houses, hear live music, and enjoy a traditional meal. Next, walk along the Malecón. It's an extra-wide walkway that goes from Old Havana to the Havana **Harbor**. The best time to go is at sunset.

Then at 9 p.m., race over to La Cabaña. At this **fortress**, you'll see soldiers dressed in uniforms from the 1700s. They shoot cannons every night to close the city gates.

Revolution Square

Callejón de Hamel

Morro Castle

You can't miss the African elements of Cuba's heritage. Cuba was once a **colony** controlled by Spain. During this time, the Spanish brought many slaves from Africa. The Africans and their **descendants** have helped shape Cuba's arts, beliefs, and food. Afro-Cuban culture is everywhere in Cuba, but one center for it is Havana's Callejón de Hamel. Dance to the rhythm of rumba music, and enjoy the colorful murals painted on walls.

Havana is a port city, so you'll spot big ships. The brave can visit the SS *San Pasqual*. This ship wrecked in 1933. It was raised from the seafloor and run aground, and now people can tour it. But many people say it's haunted!

While at the harbor, take a picture of the Morro Castle. It stands guard at the entrance to Havana Bay. Take a tour and learn about the building's history, from battling pirates to being captured in war.

Santiago de Cuba

Trinidad

Other Fun Places to Visit

Santiago de Cuba, our second-largest city, is also a port. This city was the main Spanish settlement in the 1500s. The music here should not be missed. It is the birthplace of the music called *son* (SOHN).

Visitors who don't mind getting lost can wander the twisting streets of the town of Camagüey. Centuries ago, pirates regularly raided this settlement. The villagers made their streets confusing on purpose to make it harder for the pirates to find their way around.

Trinidad is perhaps our most beautiful colonial city. Cars can't drive in the city center. That makes it a perfect place to walk. People can climb a tower for a breathtaking view!

Son musicians

Zapata Swamp National Park

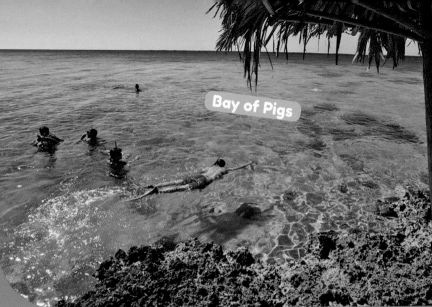
Bay of Pigs

Two-thirds of the land in Cuba is used for farming. If you visit, you'll have to find time to escape the big cities and enjoy this open countryside. Travel south and visit the Zapata Swamp National Park. It is the largest protected area in Cuba. Nearly 900 plant species and many animals are found here. If you take a tour through the park, you might spot a caimán. CHOMP! There are also a lot of other activities to do here. You can go to the beach, visit the rain forest, or enjoy a quiet day of bird-watching.

If you are in Cuba, take time to go snorkeling along the coast. You can even drink some coconut water straight out of the shell and just relax on our white sand beaches. If you happen to visit our home city of Havana, hop over to the Santa Maria Beach or Playas del Este. They are our favorite beaches here.

Our Country's History

People have lived in what is now Cuba for thousands of years. They included a variety of **indigenous** cultures and groups. Life changed dramatically when Spain made Cuba a colony in the 1500s. The Spanish enslaved or killed most of the indigenous people. They also brought deadly diseases.

As the native population fell, Spain brought slaves from Africa to Cuba. Most of the slaves worked on

Timeline: Key Moments in Cuban History

Christopher Columbus

Colonial Havana

Carlos de Céspedes

4200–2000 BCE

First Cubans

Cuba's earliest settlers make stone tools and jewelry from shells.

1492

Christopher Columbus

Sailing from Spain, Christopher Columbus lands on Cuba. Thinking he found India, he calls the people "Indians."

1500s

Spanish settlement

Spain builds its first settlement in Cuba. Spanish colonists bring the island's first enslaved Africans.

1868–1878

10 Years' War

Carlos de Céspedes leads a revolution against Spain. Slavery ends in Cuba, but the island remains part of Spain.

sugar plantations. Plantations are huge farms.

Cuba broke free from Spain in 1902, but it still struggled for independence. For many years, the United States fought to control Cuba. In the 1950s, Fidel Castro led a revolution against the U.S.-supported Cuban government. He formed the communist government we still have today. Castro was our leader until 2006. He died 10 years later.

Cuban War of Independence

Prime Minister Fidel Castro

Che Guevara

President Miguel Díaz-Canel

1895–1898

War with Spain and the U.S.
Cubans revolt. The United States and Spain fight a war. After, Cuba and other Spanish land becomes U.S. territory.

1898–1902 1906–1909

U.S. Military Occupation
The U.S. military occupies Cuba. Even after 1909, the United States interferes with the Cuban government.

1956–1959

Fidel Castro and Che Guevara
Fidel Castro and Ernesto "Che" Guevara lead a revolution against the U.S.-supported dictator in Cuba.

2014–Today

Today
Relations with the United States begin to improve. The U.S. Embassy reopens in Havana after decades of being closed.

It Came From Cuba

You won't see many cars in Cuba. Those we have are usually from the 1950s. Buying cars or car parts from other countries is against the law. We take pride in our old cars, however, and our ability to keep them running.

It's hot, hot, hot in Cuba! One way to cool down is by hopping in a *cenote* (seh-NOH-teh). It's an opening where part of the ground collapsed, revealing a natural underground pool. The cool water is ready to jump into.

Sugarcane

There is nothing tastier than a stick of raw sugarcane. Visitors traveling through should stop at one of our many sugarcane fields. Cuba is also world famous for its cigars. The cigars are handmade using a technique started hundreds of years ago.

Santería ritual

We love music in Cuba. Son is a popular style here. The main instrument in this upbeat music is the guitar. Enslaved people from Africa brought styles that still influence music today. Many use a variety of drums and other **percussion** instruments. These include the bongos, congas, and batá drums. You will also hear a lot of salsa and jazz. Get ready to dance!

Regla de Ocha, or Santería, is a religion that developed among African slaves in Cuba. Followers worship the orishas, or saints. They use percussion instruments, such as drums, during their ceremonies. This religion is passed down in spoken teachings, not written in any book.

21

Celebrate!

Everyone loves a holiday, and we have some fun ones in Cuba. Las Parrandas de Remedios is my favorite. This celebration takes place every December. It features children's parades with music, dancing, and colorful costumes. It ends on Christmas Eve with fireworks. There is even a contest between two sections of the town of Remedios. Competitors see which can make the most noise. Your parents might not like it, be we kids sure do!

Make a Tody Bird

Feel like you're in Cuba with this cute, popular Cuban bird.

Materials: tissue paper (light green, white, red), scissors, toothpick, Styrofoam ball for the head, glue, Styrofoam egg for the body, markers or crayons, pencil, mini craft sticks (1 green, 1 orange), 2 googly eyes

Directions:

1 Cut the tissue paper into small squares about 1 to 2 inches wide.

2 Poke the toothpick into the Styrofoam ball so it is half in, half out. Put glue on the other end of the toothpick and insert it into the Styrofoam egg.

3. Color the bird with markers or crayons to match the bird on page 22.

4. Fold one tissue paper square around the pencil tip. Dip it in glue and poke it into a spot on the bird's body that matches the square's color. Continue until the bird is covered with tissue paper.

5. To make the tail, insert the green craft stick partway into the Styrofoam egg, the bottom of the bird's body. Glue green tissue paper squares to it.

6. Cut the orange craft stick in half. Insert each half partway into the Styrofoam ball (the bird's head) to form the beak.

7. Glue on the googly eyes.

Let the bird dry. Then place in your room and enjoy!

February

July

September

International Book Fair
We love books! People enjoy readings by famous authors, art exhibits, and concerts.

Carnaval de Santiago:
This festival has parades, floats, fireworks, and lots of food! Join a line of conga dancers. Or sit back and enjoy the masks, giant papier-mâché figures, floats, and musicians.

Feast Day of Our Lady of Charity
This religious holiday celebrates the patron saint of Cuba. More than half of the population of Cuba is Roman Catholic, including our families.

Quinceañera
Families celebrate a girl's 15th birthday with a huge party, lots of food, a band, and a special dress for the birthday girl.

Baseball

Time to Play

Kids in Cuba love sports. Baseball is by far the favorite here. You have to go to a game if you can. There is nothing like seeing our national sport in person. Luis is the catcher on our team. I am the pitcher. Some Cubans now play in the major leagues in the United States.

Olympic boxing gold medallist

Boxing is also popular. Our boxers regularly win international competitions. So far, we have won 68 medals in the Olympics, including 34 gold!

Because we're an island country, water sports are big, too. Swimming, diving, surfing, fishing—you name it.

Dominoes

At home, my friends and I like to play *cubilete* (koo-bee-LEH-teh). This game has five dice. Each die has symbols on its six sides. These include the ace, king, queen, jack, 10, and 9. You put your dice in a cup, swirl them around, then toss them out. The goal is to get all five dice with the same symbol showing on top. Players get a certain number of points for each symbol. The ace is worth the most points. The first player to reach 10 points wins. Luis is the expert in his family, but no one can beat my grandma!

Another popular game is dominoes. You can see people of all ages playing it at home or in parks.

You Won't Believe This!

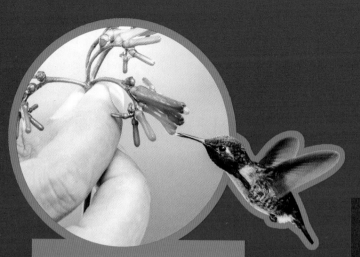

Waiting in line for eggs

The *manjuarí* (man-hwah-REE), a type of fish, is only found in Cuba. It is one of the most ancient types of fish still alive today. We also have the world's smallest bird—the bee hummingbird. It lives deep in the forest and beats its wings up to 80 times per second. The little goblin bat, Cuban jutía, and the Cuban pine toad are also unique to our country.

In Cuba, the communist government has tight control over our daily life. The government provides a certain amount of many items at a low cost, such as rice and beans. Medical care and school are also free. But you often have to wait for services. We even have a nickname for this process: *la cola cubana* (lah KOH-lah koo-BAH-nah). It means "the Cuban line."

Manjuarí

Cuba is famous for its beautiful weather. But we are also in the path of violent tropical storms and hurricanes. In 2008, five big hurricanes struck our island. In 2017, we were hit by Hurricane Irma. It was the worst hurricane to hit Cuba in 80 years. It struck the United States as well.

Drive to the Bay of Pigs and you might have to stop along the way. Sometimes huge groups of crabs fill the road as they cross from one side to the other. Talk about a fun-looking roadblock! Click. Clack. Click.

The ceiba, or kapok, tree is special to us. These giant trees grow all across the island and can live for hundreds of years. Because they can be so old, we see each tree as an important witness to history. They have experienced all the good and bad that has happened in our country.

27

Guessing Game!

Here are some other great sites around Cuba. If you visit, try to see them all!

This giant statue of Jesus overlooks the Havana Bay.

E

Play in this children's park next to huge dinosaur sculptures. Learn more about them at the nearby Natural History Museum.

A

Tourists flock to Cuba's largest offshore island, whose name translates to "Isle of Youth."

B

1. Isla de la Juventud
2. Viñales Valley Mogotes
3. Guantánamo Bay Naval Base
4. Bellamar Caves
5. Vegas Grande Waterfall
6. Christ of Havana
7. Valle de la Prehistoria

F

Travel to Topes de Collantes to view this amazing natural waterfall. Put on your swimsuit and take a dip.

Located on the eastern tip of Cuba, this navy base is controlled by the United States.

C

D

These oddly shaped hills called mogotes formed about 160 million years ago.

G

This network of caves features natural sculptures created by stalagmites and stalactites.

Answer Key

1B, 2D, 3C, 4G, 5F, 6E, 7A

28

How to Prepare for Your Visit

You might have the chance to see Cuba in person someday. Here are some tips that could help you prepare for a trip.

1 Before you come to Cuba, exchange your money. Our money is called the Cuban peso, or CUP. We also use the Cuban convertible peso, or CUC. That's the money tourists use. Most things you'll see in stores have CUC prices. Pictures of famous people and events in history decorate our money. Look on the back of the one peso bill and you'll spot Fidel Castro.

2 We greet each other with a kiss on the cheek in Cuba. Don't be surprised if we pull you in for our special way of saying "hello."

3 Cuba is warm all year. In winter and spring, it tends to be dry. Summer and fall are the country's rainy season. Hurricanes, powerful ocean storms, are most common between June and November.

4 It's best to not drink the local tap water if you are not used to it. Instead, buy bottled water, even for brushing your teeth. And remember, ice cubes are made of water!

5 There are still many limits on travel to our country from the United States. Make sure you get the proper **visa** and other travel documents. You don't want to be stuck at the airport.

6 If you need help, dial 104 for an ambulance, 105 for firefighters, and 106 for the police.

7 Slap. Smack. Smash! Make sure you bring bug spray. We have a lot of pesky mosquitoes in Cuba.

The United States Compared to Cuba

Official Name	United States of America (USA)	Republic of Cuba
Official Language	No official language, though English is most commonly used	Spanish
Population	325 million	over 11 million
Common Words	yes, **no**, excuse me, **please**, thank you	sí (SEE); **no (NO)**; perdón (pair-DOHN); **por favor (POR fah-VOR)**; gracias (GRAH-see-ahs)
Flag		
Money	Dollar	**Cuban peso (CUP) and Cuban convertible peso (CUC)**
Location	North America	Caribbean Sea
Highest Point	Denali (Mount McKinley)	Turquino Peak
Lowest Point	Death Valley	Sea level along the coast
National Anthem	"The Star-Spangled Banner"	"The Hymn of Bayamo"

So now you know some important and fascinating things about our country, Cuba. We hope to see you someday roaming through one of our colonial cities, swimming at one of our beaches, or enjoying some tasty plantains. Until then...*adiós* (ah-dee-OHS)! Good-bye!

Glossary

agriculture
(AG-rih-kuhl-chur)
the raising of crops and animals; farming

colony
(KAH-luh-nee)
territory that has been settled by people from another country and is controlled by that country

communism
(KAHM-yuh-niz-uhm)
a way of organizing the economy so that all land, property, businesses, and resources belong to the government and profits are shared by all

descendants
(dih-SEN-duhnts)
a person's children, children's children, and so on into the future

fortress
(FOR-tris)
a place such as a castle that is designed to make attack difficult

harbor
(HAHR-bur)
an area of calm water near land where ships can safely dock or put down their anchors

indigenous
(in-DIJ-uh-nuhs)
originally living in a particular area

percussion
(pur-KUSH-uhn)
a musical instrument, such as a drum, that is played by being hit or shaken

visa
(VEE-suh)
a document, usually stamped in a passport, giving permission for someone to enter a foreign country or stay there for a certain period of time

Index

Facts for Now

Visit this Scholastic website for more information on Cuba and to download the Teaching Guide for this series:

www.factsfornow.scholastic.com   Enter the keyword **Cuba**

About the Author

Michael Bell is an avid world traveler and loves to learn about and see new places. He has been interested in the history of the Caribbean, particularly Cuba, since he was a child . He grew up in Alabama, and now lives in Florida. This is his first book for Children's Press.